When The Bough Brea

CW00377122

0

When The Bough Breaks

Rockabye baby on the tree-top
When the wind blows, the cradle will rock
When the bough breaks the cradle will fall
Down will come cradle, baby and all

Is this the first recorded case of child abuse/neglect?

Prologue

The title 'When the Bough Breaks' is symbolic, to the author, of a 'breakdown' of family and/or society's care and responsibility for children.

This is the story of the author's experiences in her professional journey into social work, initially working alongside people with, what appeared to be, entrenched Victorian punitive attitudes to the treatment of perpetrators of domestic violence and, in particular, to child sexual-abusers.

The book describes changes, not only in the laws for child protection, but also in the acceptance by child-care agencies that social workers must have a recognised qualification, part of which was the introduction of psychology. This led to younger social workers with a more enlightened mind-set and to Social Work being accepted as a profession.

The cases described in this book are ones which she has found impossible to forget for varying reasons.

All names and some characteristics have been changed in order to protect identities

The Author

Jean Smith is a retired social worker (child protection officer) who practised social work from 1973-2005, initially as an unqualified social-work assistant with a Local Authority until qualifying at Bristol University, then:

1979 – 1997: the National Society for the Prevention of Cruelty to children (NSPCC), the largest child protection charity in U.K

1998 – 2000: Voluntary Service Overseas (VSO) in Russia using 'direct work' with children in a Children's Home and training psychologists in the skill.

2000 – 2005: An Independent assessor of risk for Family Courts.

In her ninetieth year, she reminisces on her years of social-work and her skills of engagement through "direct work' with children, families and perpetrators.

Other books written by the author:

My Russian Experience
The Bristol Evacuee
So! He is dead. Hallelujah

This memoir is dedicated to the un-sung heroes of social-work of every discipline who put their own welfare, mental health, even life, at risk every day due to the highly emotionally charged nature of the work .

Contents:

1.

What is Social Work: What do Social Workers actually do?

In 2014 the following Global definition of the social work profession was: approved by the International Federation of Social Workers. Switzerland

"A practice-based and academic discipline that promotes social change and development, social cohesion and the empowerment and liberation of people. Principles of social justice, human rights, collective responsibility and respect for diversities are central to social work. Underpinned by theories of social work, social sciences, humanities and indigenous knowledges, social work engages people and structures to address life challenges and enhance wellbeing

"The primary mission of the social work professional is to enhance human well-being and help meet basic and complex needs of all people, with a particular focus on those who are vulnerable, oppressed and/or living in poverty,' NASW

(National Association of Social Workers)

By empowering people to manage their own lives the skills of social workers are used in many different areas i.e., local authorities, health organisations, including NHS, voluntary organisations and charities and for private business. From the code of Ethics – BASW (British Association of Social Workers.

Some of the many tasks undertaken in their work can involve assessment, treatment, securing resources, monitoring improvement, being an advocate

2.

A foray into social-work.

In the early 1970's my interest in social work was aroused by an advert placed in the local newspaper by the Local Authority Social Services Dept for Assistant Social Workers.

I had worked for many years as a secretary to a variety of companies, lastly for a firm of solicitors.

Social work sounded 'different' and interesting. It was less pay but perhaps more rewarding?   I applied for the post and was successful.

The department was very short of social workers as many had been seconded to undertake the Certificate of Qualification in Social Work (CQSW); now a requirement to work in child protection, as recommended from the various official Enquiries into child deaths.

I was given a big caseload, consisting of elderly people, those with physical disabilities and others with learning difficulties, all classified as not needing a 'qualified' worker.

I remained in this job until 1976 when I was successful in gaining a place at Bristol University to undertake the CQSW (Certificate of Qualification in Social Work) to enable me to work with children.

In 1978, having gained my CQSW, I responded to an advert in the 'Social Work Today' magazine for the post of 'Inspector' with the National Society for the Prevention of Cruelty to Children (NSPCC) in their Bristol office.

My initial thought was "wonder what they do?"; having a vague memory from somewhere in the past of doors being kicked down and children rescued by 'The Cruelty Man.

(I remember being told by my mother that 'The Cruelty Man' once visited her family because someone had reported that their mother was always at the local pub, leaving her hungry children waiting outside for hours.

This was true, but when their mother unlocked the larder, the 'Inspector' could see that there was food, which apparently allayed his concerns and they heard no more from NSPCC)

My curiosity aroused I applied for the post which sounded attractive: a good salary, a new car every three years and a rent-free house.

Downside: a rota of week-end and once a week out-of-hours on-call duty with no overtime paid or time off in lieu. *

I was successful in gaining the post and my lime-green mini duly arrived

* The amalgamation of Child-line with NSPCC in 1989 resulted in no more unpaid out-of-hours and week-end duty for the social workers

3

Who/What is the NSPCC?

A very brief history

The National Society for the Prevention of Cruelty to Children (NSPCC) was founded in 1884 as The London Society for the prevention of Cruelty to Children by Rev. Benjamin Waugh, who had witnessed child cruelty through his work in East London. At an AGM in 1889 it changed its name to the National Society for the Prevention of Cruelty to Children (NSPCC.) Queen Victoria became the Patron with Rev. Waugh its director. The charity receives royal patronage to this day.

1889 The first act of parliament for 'The prevention of cruelty to children' commonly called 'The Children's Charter' was passed. This enabled the state to intervene for the first time in relations between parents and children. Police could arrest anyone found ill-treating a child and enter a home if a child was thought to be in danger.

1908 The Children's Act established juvenile courts and introduced the registration of foster parents.

The Punishment of Incest Act made sexual abuse within families a matter for state jurisdiction rather than intervention by the clergy

The NSPCC was and is unique amongst charities in that it has statutory powers to intervene on behalf of children in England, N. Ireland and Wales.

The Acts quoted above are just a fraction of child-care laws but the initial important ones for the NSPCC

At its outset the charity employed mainly ex-military, ex-uniformed, male personnel with a strong persona of discipline, who were then trained by the society's' own staff in their training department in London to become 'Inspectors'.

The men wore uniforms and peak caps and a 'cruelty van' was used to remove children if and when needed.

Their job was to 'inspect' allegations of abuse, mainly anonymous, by visiting the family, seeing the alleged victim and taking any action deemed to be necessary.

In 1948 Women Visitors were employed, whose main task was to take food, sympathy and/ or clothing to poor families.

At this time, 'social work' was an unknown concept.   The charity cared, and worked tirelessly for, the victims of poverty, poor housing and abuse. The focus of their intervention was mainly on working, or non-working-class families and was re-active in nature rather than pro-active.

I was told by a retired Inspector that he always took a large dog with him on investigations, making sure the dog went in first and, if he discovered that the male of the house had used violence on his wife, the Inspector warned him that if he heard of it happening again, he would ensure that the man got like-for-like, adding **"and that did the trick"**

I was also shown the log of an Inspector where he had actually punched in the face a perpetrator of domestic violence.

Victorian punitive action was deemed to be the best method of prevention, reflecting the attitude of society at that time. There was no movement to explore the reasons for, or to try to understand the root causes of, abuse/neglect.

The science of Psychology was still viewed with suspicion and mistrust and often referred to as mumbo-jumbo.

However, the winds of change were stirring, bringing recognition, as well as severe criticism, of the recurring failures of agencies to protect children and vulnerable others

The 1970's saw an era of great change in social work. After several child deaths by the hands of foster carers, an inquiry highlighted a serious lack of co-ordination among services responsible for child welfare.

Reform of child care law, with recommendations for new ones, was being pushed forward.

Reports of official enquiries led to the 1970 Local Authority Social Services Act bringing children's welfare and mental health departments together into one department, leading to the setup of Social Services Departments in England and Wales. Also, the development of Area Child Protection Committees (ACPSs) in England and Wales which co-ordinate
local efforts to safeguard children at risk

One significant recommendation from official enquiries was that social workers should be professionally trained and hold a recognised qualification.

In the 1970's discussions were underway to lobby for Social Work to be recognised as a profession as it became increasingly more obvious that it was highly related to psychology; as it remains so to this day.

The first Certificate of Qualification in Social Work (CQSW) was introduced into university curricula 1971 -1978, .to be replaced in 2003 by BA, BS or BSW in Social Work.

I had entered the profession of social work during a very interesting and progressive era.

4

Almost the start of a new career.

The wind of change impacted on the policies and practice of NSPCC as it did on all social-work child care agencies.

The need for professional training, leading to the Certificate of Qualification in Social Work, led to the realisation by NSPCC that it was going to be an extremely expensive exercise for all unqualified 'Inspectors' to continue to be paid whilst attending a qualifying course for two-three years.

The Charity relied heavily on their fund raisers to persuade the public and business to support the work they were doing and their Inspectors were required to give talks on their work to an audience of supporters

.   Rumours were rife that it was becoming increasingly more difficult to raise sufficient donations and that cut-backs were inevitable. One such cut-back was that an Inspector's rent-free property was no longer a part of the job.

The charity embarked on a recruitment drive and in1997 I was one of the first three qualified social workers to be employed straight from university, by the charity.

Part of my induction into the NSPCC meant spending nearly three months commuting to London every Monday morning and back again on Friday afternoons. A bedsit was arranged for me by the NSPCC training department.

I joined a local team of Inspectors who took me out on visits to families being supported by them, whereby I was able to get a flavour of their work.

Most of the Inspectors were also attending the training department whilst waiting for a place to be offered for the much-needed social work qualification

I was very aware that, whilst these Inspectors were dedicated to the protection of children, they had a very down to-earth approach to investigating allegations of child abuse.

Their attitude to perpetrators was punitive rather than seeking some explanation and, hopefully, helping them work towards a change of behaviour. Their knowledge was not based on psychology at that time.

I was also expected to attend lectures in the NSPCC training department and, whilst I found some of the lectures to be very interesting, particularly in child care law, I found some to be very patronising and began to question the need of being set further tests and expected to write essays on subjects I had covered for my qualification.

I was also very disturbed to discover that there were two rest rooms in the training department. One had a notice on the door stating "PQ's ONLY" (professionally qualified); their non-qualified, but-in-training, staff expected to use a separate room.

I eventually challenged the need for the setting of tests, pointing out that I had spent nearly three years of academic study and writing essays in order to prove my ability to undertake social work

The charity had employed me as a professionally qualified social worker so where was the need to continue to test me as fit for the job? It was disempowering and insulting

I refused to attend any more lectures or submit essays. The other qualified workers felt and did the same.

The lecturers seemed bemused. This stand-off was a challenge for the training staff who had been used to their prequalification students doing as they were told

A meeting was arranged with the head of the training department where opinions and grievances were aired.

Later, obviously perceived as the instigator of the 'revolt,' I was telephoned by one of the Directors to clarify my stance. He fully understood my view and agreed that the three qualified workers had been subjected to unnecessary pressure to prove, yet again, their competence.

I further expressed my disquiet at the practice in the training department of separate rest rooms for PQs and unqualified others.

I viewed this as extremely insensitive and discriminatory practice, causing resentment by the nonqualified students and embarrassment for us 'PQ's

Again, the Director, sounding surprised, agreed that the practice was demeaning, not professionally sound and would be discontinued.

It became clear that decisions made by the heads of the training department were not put to the Directors for approval; unilateral decisions were being made and put into practice, as being the way forward for the training department rather than that of the NSPCC

The training staff must have felt some disquiet at hearing the change of policy to employ already-qualified social work staff, as this was bound to impact on the work they undertook with the unqualified Inspectors. What would they do once these had gone on for professional training?

The decision made by the training 'heads' to further 'train' already qualified staff may have been viewed as the answer; a life-line; a way to ensure the continuing existence of the training department and its staff.

The 'first three' 'PQs' were guinea-pigs for the new experiment.

Our refusal to continue with the charade must have come as a shock, something that had not been foreseen or expected and must have been extremely worrying for the training staff, who projected an image of holding a very strong position of power within the charity.

The 'experiment' failed the test and proved to be the catalyst for the Directors' decision to speed up the process of qualification of their Inspectors, resulting in the inevitable closure of the London training department.

5

Now for the real start of my New Career

My three months of 'induction' were shortened and I began work in the Bristol Group office where, at that time, the main area of work was investigations of alleged physical and/or psychological abuse and monitoring families who were placed on the local authority 'at risk 'register'

The team consisted of a Group Officer, an original Inspector who had gained his CQSW, two unqualified male and one female Inspectors, all awaiting qualification training and one other qualified male Inspector; a total team of six, including me.

I was immediately given a case-load of 'at risk' cases, (children and families placed on the child protection register) at the request of child protection case conferences, which the local authority social workers were unable to deal with

. There were also many general public referrals which needed investigative follow-ups, mainly of child physical and/or emotional abuse or neglect.

Allegations of sexual abuse had to be referred immediately to the police. Neither NSPCC or the local Authority were allowed to respond to such referrals.

During my early work in Bristol, I continuously questioned why NSPCC should not be dealing with sexual abuse in the same way as any other abuse of children. The charity eventually agreed that research should be undertaken into the possibility of working in this field as well as the other abuses.

I volunteered, with five others working for the charity in different areas, to undertake a six-month study of child sexual abuse. This entailed meeting once a month, setting ourselves the task of reading whatever material on sexual abuse we could find, (which happened to be only American at that time) then sharing and re-evaluating what we had learned at the next meeting.

It was not an easy task.

My husband questioned my need to read, what he saw as, very offensive material. Furthermore, each of the study group went through phases of feeling contaminated by the material we read and not wishing to continue.

However, with the ongoing support of each other, we continued with the study which eventually took nine months to complete; at the end of which we put together a document entitled * "Developing a Child-centred Response to Sexual Abuse".

The main recommendations were that sexual abuse investigations should be carried out

21

jointly by a social worker and police person, rather than just the police, and the removal of the alleged perpetrator, pending further enquiries, rather than the child victim, as had been the practice in the past, resulting in the child believing they had done something wrong.

The document was accepted, published and printed by NSPCC and sold to other agencies. The recommended procedures were adopted by all agencies at that time.

* South- West Region Working Party (1984)
A discussion paper- London NSPCC.pp.18

The knowledge and understanding gained from this study, enabled me to become a member of the county's Area Child Protection Committee (ACPC), offering training to all disciplines in child abuse and, in particular, child sexual abuse.

I worked in Bristol for seven years: the bulk of the work for the team continuing to be that of carrying out investigations of abuse and/or neglect and heavy overwhelming case-loads of 'at risk' families/children' passed on from case conferences by the local authority.

The latter resulted in spending most of the time rushing from one case to another, just to 'monitor' in order to be able to log that you had in fact seen the child; rather than being able to use the time more productively by undertaking meaningful 'direct work' with families and/or children, to enable them to feel that they had the choice to change their way of life.

Most investigations were prompted by anonymous referrals although some came from other agencies.

The following are some examples of investigations undertaken by the author.

6

Investigations 1-4

1.

I was duty officer in my own home and at 8. p.m. received an anonymous phone call alleging a two-year-old child had been seen that day with cigarette burns on her hands, allegedly caused by her mother teaching her a lesson i.e., not to touch her cigarettes.

There was <u>always</u> a feeling of trepidation when having to carry out an investigation into an allegation of abuse and at night the trepidation was more so.   Secretly hoping that there would be no-one in and thinking of the "knocking on the door with a sponge" syndrome, explored in training.

The door was opened by a small boy. A woman shouted from the background 'Who is it – what do you want?" When I told her that I did not wish to discuss it on the doorstep she eventually came to the door.

I showed her my authorisation/identity card, and explained the reason for my visit which immediately seemed to provoke the mother into a torrent of anger and abuse, refusing to let me into the house and attempting to slam the door in my face.

(Whilst the NSPCC at that time was the only voluntary agency with the legal right to prosecute perpetrators of abuse against children, and to apply for an order to remove children to a place of safety, the Police was the only agency with the right of entry, into a property)

I quietly explained that if she refused me entry, I would have to call the police. Did she really want her neighbours to see a police car arrive? whereas my car was unmarked.

I was reluctantly allowed in; the mother continued to shout angrily, demanding to know the name of the person who had phoned me.

I pointed out that her little son was looking very worried and anxious and perhaps we should calm things down to stop him getting more upset.

The mother responded positively to my suggestion, and seemed aware of and responsive to the distress being displayed by her son.

The mother was also now showing signs off acute anxiety, pacing up and down and adamantly refusing my request to see the child. Her reason was that the child was in bed, asleep and she didn't want her to be woken up.

Whilst acknowledging her concern, I explained that my job would not allow me to leave without seeing her daughter. Continued refusal would need the involvement of the police, whereas the two of us could quietly see the child together, thereby causing as little distress as possible.

The mother, still protesting, reluctantly went upstairs with me behind her and my first misgiving was when she took a key from a pocket to unlock the bedroom door. The room had no light and there was no bulb in the fixture.

There was an overpowering smell of urine and faeces and the mother was now moaning softly, clearly very distressed and anxious. There was a muffled sound from the room

At my request the mother brought and fitted a light bulb and, as the light flooded the room, I could see a small child sitting rigidly upright, apparently having pushed herself as far as she could to the top of the bed and against the bedhead.

She looked terrified and presented with what is known as *'Frozen watchfulness/awareness'* (remaining as still and quiet as possible, on alert, whilst watching/waiting for the danger to pass.)

She was naked, except for a soaking wet and very dirty nappy and was shivering.

Talking quietly and reassuringly to the child, I softly asked the mother to get the child changed into clean clothes and to get her a warm drink. Whilst this was happening, I gently took her hands and stroked her arms, continuing to talk quietly to her until she eventually stopped whimpering.

I found, what appeared to be, cigarette burns on several fingers of one hand and on a thumb on the other. I noticed that one of her feet was badly bruised and twisted into a distorted shape.

She was noticeably under-nourished: her skin was parchment dry; her hair was very sparse and thinning, showing bald patches.

I had no doubt that this child was presenting symptoms of extreme anxiety, severe neglect/malnutrition and had been the subject of physical and, inevitably, emotional abuse.

My immediate reaction was that this child needed to be taken to be seen by a paediatrician, but it was now very dark and nearly ten-o'clock at night.

My dilemma was that removing this already traumatised child from her bed, going outside into darkness and then into a strange car by a strange person to a strange place, would surely be an additional terrifying experience for her.

She was not old enough to be given an explanation which she would understand.

The mother continued to be distressed and agitated; her behaviour now affecting her little son. He could not be left on his own and would also have to come to the hospital. The tension and stress in the home was now palpable.

I rechecked on the child who appeared to be sleeping soundly; she was warm and the light was left on a low setting.

On reaching downstairs and after a great deal of soul searching, I told the mother that, in spite of being very concerned at the poor condition of her little daughter, I had decided not to remove her that night believing that it would not be in her best interests and would cause her further stress.

I would return at 9.am the next day, hopefully with her social worker, and after ensuring that her son was in school, we would then take the little girl to the children's hospital.

As I left, the mother expressed her gratitude, tearfully, acknowledging that she badly needed help. She promised that the bedroom door would no longer be locked, having accepted the danger posed by locking such a young child in a room on her own.

She promised to check on her daughter to make sure she was no longer stressed when she went to bed herself and would be ready for me at 9.am. the next morning.

I drove home in a state of high anxiety – what if?

I firmly believed that removing a distressed child from her bed, by someone she didn't know, in the middle of a very dark night was not good practice and could not be in the child's best interest

Having assessed that she was in no more danger; another 12 hours would make little difference – hopefully!

On my return home I telephoned the Group Officer to explain what I had done and he reassured me that he respected and upheld my decision.

The next day I notified the family's social worker who met me at the house and we took the child with her mother to be examined by a paediatrician.

My initial diagnosis of malnutrition and severe neglect was confirmed and the child was admitted for further tests.   At the following child protection conference, we heard that the child's father had been physically abusive to the mother and had abandoned the family just after the little girl was born

The mother had suffered post-natal depression and, whilst the other child was well cared for, she acknowledged disliking the little girl because she looked so much like her father.

She admitted she had deliberately burned her with a lit cigarette in order to teach her not to break up her cigarettes. The twisted foot was due to her brother accidentally riding over it with his tricycle. However, no medical attention/advice had been sought; the neglect resulting in the foot being permanently disfigured.

The child was taken into the care of the local authority, and with the mother's agreement was placed for adoption.

Whilst being prosecuted for the assault on her daughter, the mother also received the ongoing help and support she badly needed

Was my decision, right? Did my intervention help?

It was not a decision I took on the spot or lightly. I had to weigh up what I believed to be in the child's best interest, against the knee-jerk panic reaction to immediately get her to hospital and, by doing so, to be seen as 'doing the right thing' and saving my skin.

The risk I took could also have impacted on my career had things gone wrong but I stuck to my professional decision.

I still firmly believe that it is not always in a child's best interest to be physically removed from their home, especially in the middle of the night.

It was not an easy decision to make and caused me a great deal of anxiety at the time.

Should the decision prove to be wrong, the welfare of a small child can weigh heavily on your conscience

.   As a social worker, you are damned if you do and damned if you do not.

The positives from my intervention were that the child was spared further abuse and neglect; while the mother received the support, she badly needed in order to deal with, and understand, her mental health issues.

When a child is the subject of abuse of any kind, it is so hard for us to understand how anyone, and a parent in particular, can harm their own child, leaving us with feelings of disgust and bewilderment.

Blame, condemnation and negative judgments do little to help the victim, perpetrator or family. Offering someone a chance to work at gaining insight into, and understanding of, their unacceptable/damaging behaviour can result in positive change for children and families.

Whilst this was an investigation with a positive outcome, a concerning factor was that the family was already known to the Social Services Dept and had been allocated a social worker.

Unfortunately, due to being overloaded with similar child-protection cases, visits were infrequent and the child and family were badly let down.

However, the existence of the NSPCC meant that there was a safety net for struggling families who were in danger of falling through the cracks of the local child protection system.

Investigation 2

A personal challenge and a dangerous stalker.

I was given a self-referral to investigate a single mother's concerns, not specified, for her eight-year-old daughter.

I was eagerly welcomed into the home by Mary very enthusiastically insisting on making me tea and constantly asking if I was comfortable. Already, I was feeling some unease, but unable to assess the reason.

The chatter was constant; about everything and nothing, except the reason for my visit. I had to stop her in mid-flow to ask for an explanation of the referral; where was her daughter? What was the problem? I began to sense that she had been drinking alcohol.

Her daughter was at school and was fit, well and happy but a demand for the payment of a gas bill had arrived that morning, throwing Mary into agitation as she was unable to find a way to pay it. She then went on to explain that this was just one of several outstanding bills.

`Whilst empathising with her anxiety I explained that my job was about protecting children from abuse and that outstanding bills did not really meet this criterion. I worked for a charity who relied on donations from the general public to continue with the child protection work so could not offer financial help.

However, on my return to the office, I would make some enquiries as to other possible helpful sources but, in the meantime, she could try the local Citizens Advice Bureau; since they were very informative about debt.

As I was leaving, her daughter came in from school. She was smiling happily, was well dressed and clearly well nourished.

Mary asked if I would come again but I explained that I didn't think it was appropriate as dealing with financial problems was not really in my remit. However, if I did find a possible source, I would write to her.

Still feeling a weird sense of unease, I closed the case as inappropriate for the agency, having checked with the girl's school who confirmed that she was a happy child, functioning well and presenting no problems.

A week later, my Group Officer gave me another referral from Mary who was requesting I visit her as she was feeling very depressed and suicidal.

I questioned the appropriateness of this but he suggested that if she was depressed it could affect the child and he wanted me to revisit and reassess although I had logged my unease.

With reluctance and an inexplicable sense of foreboding, I revisited Mary who immediately burst into tears.

She then relayed a very disturbing story of how she had got herself involved with a local sect of professional people who met on a regular basis to practise sado-masochism and that the evening before she had been seriously injured by being vaginally penetrated with instruments.

I sensed that Mary was eagerly watching for my reaction.

Trying to hide my distaste and horror I asked where her daughter was when this was going on. She was staying with her grandmother for a couple of days;the incident did not take place in Mary's home.

Again, feeling extremely uncomfortable and out of my depth, I suggested she should seek medical and perhaps psychological advice as soon as possible but that I really could not offer her any further help at this time. However, again on my return to the office I would undertake some research.

I got up to leave and as we reached her front door, she suddenly lunged toward me, pinned me against the wall and tried to kiss me. I was totally shocked and for a moment couldn't understand what was happening. Then she attempted to push her hand up under my dress.

Now terrified, and protesting loudly I push her off and ran outside to my car, quickly locking the door and starting the engine. She ran out after me and, leaning into the open passenger window, apologised profusely and pleaded with me to visit her again.

I drove home in a trance – what had just happened?

If she had been male, I would have said it was attempted rape?

When I arrived home and parked my car, I noticed something shiny on the passenger seat. It was a silver chain necklace.

The next day I relayed the incident to the Group Officer and told him that Mary was manipulating the situation and did not need social work intervention.

I did not want to visit her again.

To my amazement, he laughed and said that I should consider it to be a good character-building experience and should not be such a wimp!

I posted the planted chain back to her and closed the case once again.

Then the nightmare began

Huge bouquets of flowers were being delivered to the office addressed to me.   She telephoned me constantly several times a day.

When I protested to the Group Officer that something needed to be done, it was clear that he had no idea as to how to deal with the situation. He still seemed to think it was amusing but eventually, seeing my distress, he instructed the receptionist to refuse any more deliveries of flowers and to not put any calls from her through to me but to him.

At this time my husband was enduring a long stay in hospital and after one evening visit, I discovered Mary leaning, almost sitting, on the bonnet of my car smiling.

I angrily told her to get off but she just laughed. When I asked how she knew I would be there she said 'told you I have friends in high places.'

I drove off with her still draped across part of the bonnet until she slid off.

This was terrifying; How did she know my husband was in hospital and where to find me? Where was she getting information from? What else was she going to do?

I felt utterly helpless and fearful. Mary was obviously completely obsessed and stalking me.

A few evenings later, I was woken up by shouting and screaming outside the house. Mary was on the doorstep very drunk and my oldest son was shouting out of his bedroom window telling her to go away.

She kept screaming, saying she needed to talk to me. I refused to go downstairs, telling her from my bedroom window that I was going to call the police if she didn't go away. She was begging me to go down to see her.

Fortunately, I had a phone connection in my bedroom and rang the police who arrived very quickly. I could hear them telling her to calm down and move on otherwise she would be arrested.   She continued to protest so she was taken off in the police car

I cannot begin to explain the fear I felt for me and my family that night and the sheer hopelessness of the whole situation which no-one seemed to take seriously.

When would it end?

That was the question that I would ask again and again.

A week later I had a phone call at home in the evening from my area manager asking me to meet him in the Group Office immediately to answer a complaint made against me.

Mary had written to the NSPCC headquarters in London alleging that she had had an affair with the Bristol Inspector. The allegation was passed on to the Area Manager who had visited her in her home and taken a statement.

I listened in shock but not surprise. She alleged that she had had the best sex ever with me several times but that I was now rejecting her. She was angry at the rejection and wanted revenge. She expressed wanting me sacked.

Her word against mine!

Had he read my very thorough case recording in which I had told of my concerns.? Had he read about her assault/attempted rape. Had he read about the stalking with flowers, phone calls and following me around? Had he read about the intimidation of me and my family?

Her word against mine!

I was suspended pending a full review.

Two days later I received a phone call from one of the Directors of NSPCC

Further enquiries revealed that Mary had a history of alcoholism and bizarre, almost psychotic behaviour resulting in police involvement in the past She had had, and was again receiving, psychiatric treatment and support

Mary had written to the NSPCC London Headquarters again admitting that she had lied because of, her perceived, rejection by me. She now wished to retract her complaint.

Great! Mud sticks – what now?

The Director expressed his sympathy and apologised for the lack of management understanding and appropriate support.

Would I like to move away to another area team with all expenses covered?

I declined.

Why should I be expected to uproot my family to go to an unknown area, our lives turned upside down, because of poor, unprofessional management?

The outcome of this investigation did not feel good or positive but is an example of the potential risk taken by social workers when undertaking the unknown in good faith.

The fact that a manager perceived an assault on me by a woman as amusing and 'character building' was staggeringly myopic and, in my view, totally unprofessional.

Would he have reacted in the same way if the assailant had been male?

Investigation 3

A desperate plea for help from a woman with two small sons who was in fear of her husband.

She requested a specific date and time for a visit when her husband would not be home

Alice lived with her family in a remote cottage. Her husband Brian worked long hours as a farm hand.

Recently Alice had become increasingly aware of her husband's very controlling attitude. He was constantly criticising her; the food she cooked, the way she dressed, the way she looked. When she tried to talk to him, he was dismissive. Alice felt that she could do nothing right and her self-esteem had hit rock bottom resulting in a lot of weeping which Brian also used to taunt her as an example of her weakness. (a clear indication of a controlling narcistic personality)

Alice didn't drive and the country buses were very infrequent. However, she made an effort when the boys had gone to pre-school to take a bus to the nearest shopping area just to get out of the house and see other people.

This was now becoming more difficult because of her husband's objections and instructions that she should stay at home.

There were no near neighbours or family support as Brian's attitude had made her parents feel very unwelcome.

I had a long discussion with Alice, suggesting she think carefully about what she wanted to happen. She said that all she could think about was to take her sons and move to somewhere where she would feel safe.

She didn't want to involve the police and was in a confused state of high anxiety, searching desperately for a way out.

We talked about the possibility of a women's' refuge and that I would make enquiries after this visit and get back to her in a day or so. In the meantime, she should start to think about what she might need to take with her and how she would explain a move to her children.

On getting back to the office, I immediately phoned around various refuges and Alice's name was put on their list. If and when a vacancy occurred, the refuge would contact me immediately

On my second visit to Alice and her children she relayed that recently his attitude towards her had become threatening. He had taken his shot-gun out of the cabinet, loaded it and now kept it in clear sight near him.

Although she had had no previous concerns about her children being in danger from their father, she expressed being worried that they may be emotionally upset by the hostile atmosphere in the home.

I told Alice that if she was really frightened by another incident, she must try to ring the police or me and I would visit the local police station.

As usual, I recorded these events on the file which resulted in my Group Officer 'ordering' see him in his office. He had the file in front of him and having read the shot-gun episode, told me that I must go back immediately and confront Brian about his actions and inform the police.

I was staggered and refused; explaining that I had supported Alice to the point when she was ready to move out with her sons, as and when the occasion safely arose. If I were to confront Brian, he would know that Alice had informed about the gun and would probably guess that she was planning to leave him.   The whole carefully orchestrated plan would be thwarted and an extremely dangerous situation could occur.

 'If you are refusing to carry out an order, I shall ring Headquarters'

I confirmed my refusal.

He rang London and spoke to one of the Directors who asked him to pass the phone to me.

I explained that I was working with the mother to get her and her sons out of a difficult, possibly dangerous, situation which needed to be done delicately and tactfully.

I would not confront someone with a shot gun, putting my life, and others, at risk.

Arrangements were in hand to help this family; Confrontation with the father at the moment was not in the best interests of the children or their mother.

Tutting loudly, the Director agreed with me and requested that the phone be passed back to the Group Officer who sheepishly withdrew his 'order' and discussed the situation, sensibly, with me.

After much planning and support to enable Alice to stay strong in her resolve to move away from the dangerous situation, I was able to help her and her children move into a women's refuge where they received the support and encouragement needed to change their life for the better.   I have used this case as an example of some of the bullying and authoritarian attitudes that were still in practice by some of the previous 'Inspectors'. Even though they had trained and qualified as social workers, they were still entrenched in 'confrontation and punishment' rather than empathy and understanding, or in accepting using the science of psychology as a factor, leading to potential treatment.

Investigation 4

An anonymous referral alleging children were living in squalor
I checked the 'at risk' register. The family name was not registered but known to local social services.

I phoned but the social worker was not available, neither was the SSD team manager. So, I visited.

The door was opened slightly but with difficulty by a small child. I could just see a little face peering at me through the narrow gap.
A woman's' voice in the back ground asked what I wanted.

Me '*I can't explain from here*

She shouted for me to push the door hard but something was stopping it from opening.

It scraped back an inch or two as I pushed my whole body against it and I could just see through the gap. A small child standing in the hallway. I pushed harder and was eventually able to enlarge the gap and squeeze through.

There was an unbelievable mountain of 'things' stacked up behind the door, almost to the top; magazines, papers, tins bottles jars, clothing, shoes, plates, mugs, toys etc. The rubbish spewed over into the living room; I couldn't find a space to put my feet. I could see a sofa piled with 'stuff' and rubbish crammed underneath it.

There were piles of clothing on every chair and surface. There were mattresses on the floor. The only floor spaces free of rubbish were covered with animal excrement The house was stinking.

There was a baby asleep in a pram in one corner of the room. Mother was sitting on a chair with a toddler on her lap. She looked unkempt, unwashed and with matted hair.

I was initially speechless, in shock. The mother seeing the look on my face started to weep. I immediately reassured her that we will get things sorted and asked her if I could make her a cup of tea, but there was no tea bags or milk. The two other children were equally unkempt and looked hungry.

Talking to her gently I asked what had happened. She explained that since having the baby a couple of weeks previously she hadn't been able to shop or clean or even leave the house but she didn't understand why.

The mattresses on the floor were there for them all to sleep together because the bedrooms were so cold and in a mess. She didn't know where to start.

I asked if I could go upstairs. She nodded.

There was cat and dog excrement on every stair and in every room, with evidence of a child walking through it at some time. There was also human excrement smeared on some of the bedroom walls. Every room was cluttered with 'stuff'

The mother told me that a social worker had visited her some time ago.

I explained that I was going to see her social worker straight away and that she and the children would be taken to a clean house and given food. Her home would be cleaned up and repainted so that they would all be able to go back home again.

She was sobbing uncontrollably and the two children looked bemused. She said she felt ashamed. I told her that I thought she was suffering from post- natal depression and had stopped functioning, but it wasn't her fault.

I shopped and left her some milk and food for them all and drove to the local social services department where I was told again that the social worker was not available. I requested to see her manager.

Some local authority team leaders/managers showed hostility to any intervention by NSPCC and this particular one extremely so.

When I explained the reason for my visit his staggering response was "Well what do you expect **me** to do about it? The social worker will sort it out when she gets back."

I took a deep breath "*Well, if you are going to do nothing about it today, then I must do something.*

He asked me if I was threatening him? (I guess I was). I reiterated that no child should be left in such squalid conditions for another minute and if he was going to do nothing then I would visit the local police station, request a joint visit by an officer and between us we would make sure those children were removed to a place of safety.

It worked. He told me that he would go to see himself and sort it out and would ring my Group Officer with the outcome and complain about my attitude!

A few days later the social worker for the family came to the office to tell me that she wanted to thank me for my intervention. It had taken three skips to clear the rubbish from the house.

44

The family was placed in temporary accommodation while the house was being cleaned and repainted. She had taken the mother to see her GP who had confirmed a diagnosis of post-natal depression and prescribed anti-depressants.

The family social worker admitted feeling that she had failed the family. She had not realised that the mother was not functioning and she, the social worker, had stopped seeing the chaos in the home
. She had been anxious not to be viewed as judgmental by using her own middle-class values to judge how others should live.

Did she really think that working-class people lived in such chaos; did she believe that this was the 'norm' for that class?

She looked very embarrassed and agreed with me that no child, of whatever class, should have to live in such degradation. She expressed feeling ashamed that she had let the family down. She also apologised for the reception I had received from her manager.

A positive outcome for the family and perhaps a lesson in humility for their support worker.

Again, this highlighted the importance of the existence of the NSPCC.

When the local authority Social Services were unable to respond, probably due to the pressure of child protection work, the NSPCC could provide a service.

Unfortunately, the NSPCC was not always welcomed

by social-work managers, particularly when the involvement of the charity may highlight shortcomings in child-protection services.

The very word 'charity' in itself, is indicative of a failure by governments to provide care and protection adequality for its citizens.

7

Moving to another area and 'Direct Work'

My continuing frustration at not being able to use the skills I had, together with the lack of good management support, spurred me into applying for a position of child protection officer in an NSPCC special unit in another county.

My application was accepted and I was able for the next eleven years to practise my skills of 'direct work' with children and families and also with perpetrators of child-sex abuse.

This was definitely a good move with exciting projects arising.

I was afforded the opportunity to attend a two-week course at the NSPCC Gilmore training Centre in Leicester, leaving with a 'Trained Trainer' certificate. The course was useful in helping to focus on the practicalities of putting together professional courses from beginning to assessment. The team was very proactive in running courses for other disciplines on all categories of child abuse, so my further skills in this area were of use.

It was the time when child sexual abuse was really making the headlines in social work. My previous nine-month study of the subject would now be an asset and most of my future work was focused in that area, either with victims or perpetrator

8

Working with victims of child sexual-abuse 1-2

The dreaded question   *

<u>"If I tell you a secret, will you promise not to tell?"</u>

Stomach churning; cold fear sweeping over me, clutching at my heart which, for a second, stops beating, then races, blood pounding through my veins knowing, dreading what is to come.

Shall I change the subject, I really do NOT want to know. Maybe it isn't a bad secret that she desperately wants to share: my senses on alert, fully aware of the possible ensuing hell. dread or shock: just listen intently

I know in my heart that the child wants "it" to stop and only telling will enable the beginning of that stop; but at what cost? I fear, it will be dear.

The consequent hell of broken trust, frightening interviews with police and social worker, intrusive medical examination, the probable break up of family, torn apart by the never-to-be spoken, unbelievable, unthinkable, difficult to comprehend things to be heard; will this child's nightmare be believed?

Will the child and family be punished, perhaps losing the breadwinner, their home, friends, neighbours.

The feeling of guilt felt by a victim for the consequences, weighing heavily; the confusion of still feeling love for the perpetrator but hating what was done

My inner self is screaming   <u>Please do not tell me your secret.</u>

The professional worker has to say

"Because my job is to protect you, if you tell me of something that is making you feel uncomfortable, perhaps harming you, something that we both know should not be happening, I have to tell others in order to get it to stop and keep you and others safe. I'm guessing you want it to stop too and that is why you want to share your secret

*A poem penned by the author some years ago.

Case 1

I am attending a multi-agency child protection case conference, consisting of representatives from local Health, Police, Education, and Social Services Departments.

We are all aware of some of the concerns behind the reason for the conference and are now listening intently, silently; the occasional gasp or short intake of breath to be heard coming from incredulous listeners, breaking the silence as the sorry tale unfolds.

Two years previously, a young girl in the local junior school had asked the school nurse to promise to keep a secret she wanted to tell her. Naively, the nurse did so, thereby enabling the ongoing sexual abuse of two young children for another two-three years......

That young girl eventually showed all the signs of pregnancy and revealed that her father had sexually abused her for several years

A joint investigation was carried out by police and social workers, resulting in the arrest and removal to prison of the girl's father, her mother and mother's cohabiter both living next door to the girl. Their 4-year-old son was taken to a place of safety with foster carers.

An older sister had also been sexually abused by their father many years earlier and was living with him and their child as a family, the abuse unknown to the authorities until the recent investigation.

Both families had 'inter-swapped' sexual partners, including their children and animals, all becoming part of a wider local net-work of child sex- abusers.

It was discovered that the mother had been a willing participant in the historic abuse of her two daughters by their father and the next-door neighbour.

She had left her two daughters with their abusive father to live next door with her neighbour by whom she had a son.

She now appeared to be relieved to tell of her current involvement, along with her partner, who she blamed, for the sexual abuse of their young son, now nearly four years old.

The most horrifying thing that I had heard in my eighteen years of experience as a child protection officer and in my work with abused children was that of the involvement of a six-month-old baby boy in sexual activity with his parents and animals.

The child, now nearly four years old, became inappropriately sexually stimulated by scenes of affection or partial nudity he witnessed on TV or otherwise. His foster carer reported that he was over-interested in her young daughter getting undressed for bed and wanted to touch her private parts.

He would become sexually aroused resulting in him masturbating to the point of soreness.

Recommendations of the conference were that the adults would all be registered as sex offenders, the daughters and their children would be placed on the child protection register with support from Social Services.

It was further recommended that Frankie should be given a period of work therapy "**In order to normalise his behaviour**" and I was asked to undertake this work.

I remember driving back to the office in a state of shock, bewilderment and almost panic.   How do you "normalise" behaviour which has been "normal" for four years?

How do you explain "normal" to a four-year old? Where would I start? What special tools were available?

So many questions and no-one had any answers at that time. Who could/would guide me?

My place of work was an ex-army officer's house, allocated to NSPCC rent free in return for offering "work" when necessary to M.O.D. personnel

We were officially known as the NSPCC special unit/child therapy centre in which had been constructed a playroom on the ground floor which consisted of a play kitchen and various books and toys.

I worked in a team of six child protection officers plus a manager. We specialised in training other social workers and multi-agency staff across the county in child protection issues.

We also specialised in investigating all child abuse categories and I had a special skill in working in the area of child sexual abuse.

We had recently bought the new sensational 'Anatomically Correct Dolls" (A.C) which caused great amusement initially

A father, mother, son and daughter dolls, all with oral and anal openings, ears, tongues, nipples, hands with individual fingers for all and a vagina, clitoris and breasts for the female doll and a penis and testicles for the male doll.

We also had recently invested in recording equipment. All useful in investigations and perhaps now in therapeutic work.

Would they be of use, a help, in 'normalising' Frankie's behaviour?

It had been agreed that Frankie would be picked up from the foster carer and brought to the centre by his social worker for an hour's session every week for six weeks.

After discussion with other members of the team, it became clear that no-one had any idea of what or where to go with the proposed sessions.

I was on own with this one so recording the sessions would be vital for re-evaluating the content and progress of each session, providing a chance to put right any mistakes.

I had decided the first session would be a fairly brief introduction to me and the surroundings for Frankie and that I would try to go at his pace and pick up on his body language as to how comfortable or uncomfortable he was feeling.

Session 1

Frankie arrived; a small blond, rather fragile child, looking perplexed, anxiously clinging to the hand of his social worker who, I suggested, should stay with us for this first session.

We toured the room, examined the various pieces of equipment, toys etc then a run around in the garden after which a drink of squash with biscuits was eagerly welcomed.

I explained to Frankie that I was hoping to help him with the puzzle of why mum and dad were no longer at home and why Frankie was living with Mrs. E, but we would not start until next week when we might do some crayoning, have a drink and more biscuits.

Frankie seemed to be reassured and said he would like to come again next week.

After he had left, I telephoned the foster carer to explain what we had done and asked her to let me know how he reacted when he reached her home. I also requested that she tell me of any concerns which may occur in the meantime before I meet with him again.

PHEW! Relief, it was over. I think it went well, but nothing was really 'done'. Not sure what I expected.

What to do on the next session?

Must try to think like Frankie.

What must he have felt when police cars raced to his house and rushed into his home.

I assumed, very Scared and extremely confused.

Why did the policemen take mum and dad away and where are they?

Why did the social worker take him to Mrs. E's home? Had anyone explained things to him?

I felt that this was a good base to start – let's take him through the process of that traumatic day.

Session 2

Frankie arrived looking relaxed, happy for his social worker to wait in the office this time and he opted to go out into the garden for a while before we started some "work".

I made a long road out of pieces of paper on which Frankie's house was drawn as well as a police station and another house to represent the foster carer, Mrs. E and placed the road on the floor

. I explained that I we were going to try to help both of us understand what had happened on the day the police came to his house and suggested we have a rummage in the toy box to see if we could find a police car and a policeman, which we did.

Can Frankie make a noise like a police car? *Yes, 'neenaw neenaw'* very loudly as we drove the police car along the paper road until it stopped at Frankie's house.

Out jumped our play policemen and went into Frankie's house. Frankie was scared and didn't know what was happening –

Mummy was screaming and Daddy was swearing and shouting. Frankie was crying in the corner.

The policeman pushed Mummy and Daddy outside

Frankie was taken outside into a car and taken with a social worker in her car to the house of Mrs. E

At this point Frankie was clearly upset.

Would he like a cuddle? He nodded, after which we stopped for a drink and biscuits. I asked Frankie if he would like to finish for today and perhaps continue the next time he came.

Another nod, so the session was ended.

I phoned Mrs. E to explain what we had done, what had been said, and that he was a little subdued. She told me that he was still masturbating, making himself sore and she wasn't sure how to deal with it.

I suggested that she get him to, or let her, put some cream on his sore bits whilst explaining that the rubbing was making him sore, so it was not a sensible thing to do. Also, if she saw him start to become aroused, to try to divert his attention to something else but not to make him feel guilty.

Frankie's body had been inappropriately sexually stimulated from such a young age that it was now "natural" for his body to respond to visual or contact stimuli and become aroused easily. Being so young meant that he had not been able to learn the skills of control and had not been taught strategies to avoid or deal with an erection.

Whilst his body responded automatically to stimuli, it was not developed enough to allow ejaculation, therefore masturbation gave him no sense of relief/release and resulted in soreness.

Hopefully; this could be explained to him at some point in the future when he was old enough to understand the workings of his own body

Session 3

In the last session Frankie and I had started to explore what had happened on the day his parents had been arrested but Frankie had become upset so the session was shortened.   Hopefully we would be able to expand on this subject in this session

Frankie came into the play room happily and immediately asked for a drink. Whilst sitting down together for the drink and biscuits I asked Frankie if he remembered what we had done last time.

He got the police car out of the play box; he remembered playing with this and that it went to his house and took Mummy and Daddy away.

Shall we find out where they went? Frankie showed no reluctance or anxiety to go over the scene again; he neenawd, neenawd, pushing the car to his house

We acted out his parents being driven off, stopping at the police station. Did Frankie know why?

No.

The police thought that Mummy and Daddy may have done something very naughty and needed to talk to them at the police station.

Frankie hadn't been naughty but needed to go to Mrs. E's house to be looked after until Mum and Dad could go back home.

The play acting ended. I tentatively asked Frankie if he understood what we had just done and he responded by asking when his parents would be back home with him.

57

I quietly explained that they had to stay in the police station until a judge said it was ok for them to go home, but this might not be for a long time. In the meantime, Frankie would be kept safe with a foster carer.

I sensed Frankie's distress. It was so important to go softly, softly with him, to go at his pace and not push an agenda.

At age four there was a limit to what he could absorb and understand. A hug? Yes

Then time for biscuits and squash.

Frankie left with his social worker, a little quiet this time but said happy to come next week.

Time for me to reflect on what had been covered so far, examining Frankie's reactions very carefully in order to keep in step with his understanding.

Contact with Mother

The court had conceded to Frankie's mother's request to have supervised contact with him once a month in a neutral setting and the NSPCC child centre had been agreed.

I sat in with them initially but it became clear that his mother was more interested in talking to me than interacting with her son.

I learned that she felt privileged to have the "third eye" on her forehead which, she seemed to think, somehow excused her behaviour of involving her son in sexual activities when, at only 6 months old, she performed oral sex on him whilst engaging sexually with her partner. They both encouraged Frankie when he was older to try to penetrate his mother and a rabbit.,

Not wishing to hear any more I decided to leave Frankie with his mother for a short time whilst I monitored the recording.

She just sat passively, flicking through a magazine, not interacting at all with Frankie. There was no conversation or cuddles and at one point I could see Frankie trying to get into the toy washing machine, probably through boredom and getting no response from his mother.

I returned to the play room and asked her if she had noticed that Frankie was trying to get into the washing machine and why did she think he did this?

She reacted surprised when I suggested that he was clearly trying to get her attention without success.

59

Session 4

A happy Frankie arrived and I started to talk about mum and dad.

How about you show me what they look like on these big pieces of paper. Can you draw me a picture of Mummy and Daddy?

I had found some old wallpaper and felt tips and with no hesitation Frankie enthusiastically got down to drawing as I watched, quietly, with no input, fascinated at what was emerging.

Both parents were depicted as very large outlines, almost filling a space 22" square – both figures totally nude.

Dad with arms outstretched, the width of the paper and a penis reaching to the ground, a powerful, dominant image.

Mum, a very large, round. obese figure with huge dangling breasts and a red star shape in the middle of her forehead.

Frankie finished with a flourish and looked up at me excitedly, clearly pleased with his work and waiting for my reaction.!

We both sat back to admire the finished work and Frankie was smiling

Caught on the hop! *"Well, those are very good pictures Frankie. Dad has very long arms.* I used the opportunity to test out his knowledge/terminology for their anatomy

Can you tell me what this is? (Pointing to the male penis)

Daddy's willy'

Ok. can you show me Mummy's willy?

There! (Jabbing between her legs). *but it's not a willy, it's a mini.*

Ok. What do you call these big things here?

Titties

Ok. Thank you, Frankie.

And what do you call this (the mark on her forehead)

Mummy's *other eye.*

Do you think we should give mum and dad some clothes? (Careful! mustn't let Frankie think there is something wrong in going around the house in the nude)

They can't get on a bus or go shopping like that can they? And it is very cold today. Frankie nodded.

What shall we give dad? Pants to cover his willy and perhaps trousers and a shirt.

I drew something on some coloured paper that looked a bit like these garments, cut them out and Frankie helped glue them onto the figures.

What about Mummy? We cut out pants and a dress and Frankie stuck them on.

A happy Frankie enjoyed his biscuits and drink and left with his social worker looking pleased.

I phoned Mrs. E to let her know of the content of the session as there might be some reaction. Again, reminding her to always make sure that Frankie was not left alone with her small daughter.

Frankie had also inappropriately touched the private area of the dad of the house in an effort to please. A strong message re. privacy was needed.

On reflection I felt that this was a positive session and that we were moving slowly-but-surely to the nitty-gritty subject, with Frankie now taking the lead, which was encouraging,

Session 5

It had now become the norm for Frankie to bounce into the play room, eager to explore the toy boxes and make his own decision as to what we might play with.

We started this session with biscuits and a drink and I; enquired how he was, what life was like at Mrs E's etc.

Frankie responded appropriately whilst diving into the various boxes.

I was suddenly aware that Frankie had pulled out the A.C dolls and was examining each of them intently, pushing his finger into the various orifices.

He suddenly turned the mother-doll figure onto her face and was holding the boy-doll figure over her, and pulling on the little penis.

Taken aback, I looked up quickly to see if the tape was running. It was!

Can you tell me what you are doing Frankie?
Sex – this is sex

What are you doing that is sex
Putting his willy in
Why are you doing that?
Dad said
"What did Dad say?"
You better do it Frankie; you better do it.
Frankie then demonstrated that the mother doll should be on her hands and knees and Dad would hold the boy to stand on her legs. Dad would rub the boy's willy and push it into mummy.
What happens after this sex Frankie?
I get presents sometimes but my willy hurts.
Taking a deep breath, I gently explained that what Mum and Dad were doing, what they had done to and with him, was very naughty.
Sex is for grown-ups and not for children
It was very naughty if grown-ups did sex with children. It was not a good thing for children to do sex and that is why his willy gets very sore.
That is why mum and dad had to go to court and then prison because they did naughty things to you and your sisters which hurt you and them.
You and your sisters have done nothing wrong but mummy and daddy should not have done sex with you or them.
Shall we tell them Frankie? Frankie nodded:

Taking each doll in turn I told-off Mummy and Daddy for doing sex with Frankie and his sisters.

63

Mummy and Daddy then said to the children-dolls that they had been very naughty and were sorry that they made them do sex.

The atmosphere was sad. I hesitated to ask Frankie at this point if he wanted a hug but gave him the choice. He shook his head.

So, I thanked him for his hard work, then chocolate biscuits and squash.

As Frankie was leaving with his social worker, he turned, came back and gave me a hug.

I needed that, and I guess he did too.

Some of the team were watching the recording and were totally surprised and shocked by what they had witnessed and heard, as was I, but also relieved that Frankie had precipitated the opportunity for me to face and deal with the difficult subject at last.

Session 6

We had a good walk around the garden then sat under the tree for a while, Frankie was aware that this was our last session and asked if he could come again,

I Explained that his social worker knew how hard Frankie had worked to tell us what had happened at home and he would help Frankie in the future.

I brought the sessions to an end by a fairly simple recapping to see what Frankie had absorbed.

He knew that Mummy and Daddy had been naughty by doing sex with him

Do you know why that was naughty Frankie?

Because 'grown-ups shouldn't do sex with children'

Well done, Frankie

I checked out Frankie's vocabulary for genitalia, explaining that there are many other different words that people use, whatever makes them feel comfortable. I explained the correct terminology, but I also called them 'Private parts'

We talked about these private bits of the body and what this meant. No-one should touch those private parts without permission and certainly not if it made us feel uncomfortable.

As an example, I spoke of his wanting to touch the 'mini' of the little girl in Mrs E's home.

She didn't want him to do this. It was 'private' and no one must touch her in that way except her mother or maybe a doctor or nurse.

Children must not touch, or be asked to touch the private parts of grown-ups as this could be dangerous for children.

It was very difficult trying to help Frankie deal with arousal as this had become a normal reaction over which he had little or no control; but he knew that an erection made him feel uncomfortable and that rubbing himself just made his willy very sore.   Until he was a few years older, arousal did not result in pleasure.

Perhaps he could tell Mrs. E when his willy was getting hard and she might be able to take his mind off it by engaging him in some other activity.

I had already made this suggestion to Mrs. E. and it was beginning to work quite well.

Touching on Frankie's family was also very difficult. The relationships were so complex and confusing. Frankie had two half-sisters whose children were his nieces, but their father was also their grandfather and their grandmother was Frankie's mother.

My task of endeavouring to "normalise" Frankie's behaviour was complete but I will probably never know if it was successful.

I can only hope that I helped Frankie understand the reason for his parents being imprisoned and him having to live with a carer.

I hope that the work we did together had an impact on his understanding and that I did not make him feel any guilt.

I truly hope that Frankie was able to reach an understanding of his body and sexuality and eventually to lead a 'normal', happy, sexual life in future

Two or three years after my work with Frankie, I had a phone call from his social worker to say that he was engaging Frankie in drawing up his 'world' and the important people in it. Frankie wanted to put my name in his 'world 'but his social worker needed to ask my permission which, of course, I gave

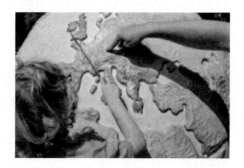

What a reward! Frankie viewed me as a person worthy
enough to be part of his world.

Case 2

An eight-year-old girl was referred to me for therapeutic input after her father had been sent to prison for sexually abusing her.

Felicity was the younger of two daughters living with both parents and it was thought she had been inappropriately touched by her father for several years

I visited Mrs. C who became very upset, explaining that. she and her husband had been happily married for fifteen years. When Felicity told her that she didn't like dad tickling her, she initially laughed – dad and Felicity had always been close and there was a lot of tickling.so it was not a problem. She would tell dad to stop the tickling.

(I had previously come across several cases where 'innocent' tickling of a child seemed to be viewed as the way in to gain a child's trust before the onset of sexual abuse. The child always expressed feeling uncomfortable but not knowing how to stop it.)

Mrs. C. had sensed that Felicity was much quieter than normal, seemed to be holding back, hesitating, and looked distressed. With her mother's reassuring cuddle, she was able to tell the full story.

The tickling had progressed from under-arm and tummy tickling when dad tucked her in bed, to tickling her vagina. Feeling confused and uncomfortable Felicity did not know what she should do.

Nothing was said for a while, then dad had asked her to touch his private parts and Felicity expressed feeling scared. To be told that someone you have lived with for years, someone you love and trust, someone you believe you know better than anyone else, has been sexually abusing a child, <u>your daughter,</u> must be the most earth-shattering, devastating, unbelievable news ever to be heard.

Unfortunately, a lot of women cannot, or refuse to, believe this of their partner, leaving the child feeling guilty and abandoned.

Thankfully, Mrs. C believed her daughter, a quiet, rather reserved child, the exact opposite of her outgoing, fun-seeking older sister who hadn't had the same experience – why?

There was the clue. Fun-seeking, outward-going children rarely become the victims of abuse because their nature would probably mean challenging any behaviour which made them feel uncomfortable.

Victims of sexual abuse are usually quiet in demeanour and present as vulnerable.

The family was in shock and crisis. There had been the inevitable investigation and the father had been imprisoned.

The imprisonment of the bread winner caused financial difficulties and neighbourhood gossip impacted on their lives. The sister was angry initially with Felicity, adding to her distress and feelings of guilt.

Felicity had become more reserved and spent a lot of her time in her bedroom weeping.

Mrs. C agreed, with Felicity's consent, to bring her to see me for three weekly sessions of up to an hour Felicity had already been through the gruelling, embarrassing, distressful process of an investigation into the abuse she had experienced by her father. She would have reluctantly had to have undergone a physical examination and then try to find words, through tears, in order to tell the policewoman and social worker the details of that abuse. She may have had to do this more than once,

I would not put her through that yet again unless she specifically requested doing so.

My work with her would be to give her a chance to talk about her family, her network of friends in and out of school, and to examine and hopefully express her feelings

Session 1

Felicity was withdrawn on arrival, clearly anxious and nervous

I asked if she would like to see the office where I worked and then the work room.   This seemed to break the ice and after the tour we had biscuits and drinks.

I explained to Felicity that we were not going to talk about what had happened, unless that was what she wanted. I would like her to tell me about her family and how she saw her position in it. We started by drawing up a basic tree on a large piece of paper, with her guidance.

She hesitated at one point and then asked me if it was ok to put her father on the tree.

Would she like him to still be in the tree?

A pause. She was clearly thinking about this, then said

Yes, but not yet

That's fine; perhaps we can talk about that again another time.

We continued to fill in the tree with her extended family of grandparents etc on either side of the family. They had all been quite close but Felicity felt things had changed since the 'problem' in that the extended family were also finding it difficult and not visiting

We touched on her immediate friends and again Felicity was able to say that she felt her friends had become distant.

Felicity was upset. *would she like a cuddle? A* shake of the head. *Shall we finish for today?* A nod. The session over, I emphasised to Felicity that she was not to blame for what had happened and perhaps we could talk a little more about that next week. Another nod.

Session 2

Felicity less nervous and with a smile on her face. Squash and biscuits and checking on how she had been since I last saw her, she replied 'O.K.'

Recapped on the tree and Felicity's feelings that things had changed with the extended family.

71

We focussed on Felicity's relationship with her immediate family members. She expressed feeling' a bit close' to her sister whom she saw as a much stronger person than herself. *Do you think that that relationship had changed too?*

Yes,

Her sister was angry with Felicity at first and didn't believe the thing about their dad but she did after a talk with mum.

What about your relationship with mum?

No that hasn't changed. At first, she said she couldn't believe it but then she did.

Well, that's because she is a very caring and loving Mum and is also feeling bad about what happened to you. She feels guilty too that she didn't know sooner

But Mum didn't know because I always liked dad putting me to bed until…………

……*Felicity, the bad things that happened to you were not your fault, or the fault of your Mum. Dad is a grown-up and knew he should not have touched you in the way he did. He knows that sex is for grown-ups not children. You were very brave to have told mum.*

Felicity is distressed *Ok do you want to stop now and see what happens next week?* Yes

Allowing the child to go along at their own pace is essential in order to alleviate further stress. Felicity needed to be able to talk about her feelings with no pressure exerted by anyone.

72

I had had a conversation with Felicity's mum after each session so that she was aware of what her daughter might be feeling.

After the last session Mrs C. expressed feeling some relief that Felicity seemed to be less 'low' now that she had started to talk about her feelings.

Session 3

Felicity's last session was a recoup on all we had touched on up to the point of talking more about her father.

Yes, she was always very close to him   He tucked her up every night into bed and used to read her stories. He told her some times that he felt sad and Felicity would then give him an extra cuddle on the bed.

She had never really liked being tickled., It aways made her feel uncomfortable, especially as she got older and her top bit got bigger. Dad would sometimes laugh and touch her there, saying his little girl was growing into a lady.

Felicity wasn't sure if she liked him saying that and really didn't like him touching her there, but didn't like to upset him by saying so.

Then the touching became more worrying; Dad told her it was because he loved her so much; much more than her sister who would be jealous, so she mustn't say anything.
She was his very special girl.

But now her dad was in prison and she missed him. Her mother was always crying and her sister wasn't the same to her

I wish I hadn't told <u>anyone</u>
Such a heart-breaking plaintiff cry.
She needed a hug.

Holding her tightly, I explained that her whole body
was telling her that what dad was doing was wrong but she
was confused because he told her all the time that he loved
her and wouldn't hurt her. She had trusted him. He was her
dad and dad's do not do that to their daughters.
But her dad did!
It was not her fault. He was a responsible adult and
she was only a child with no power to stop what was
happening without telling someone;
She had been very brave and had done the right
thing to get it stopped so that she would no longer be abused
and she helped her father get what help he might need.
I sensed that this last remark helped her feel better. I
told her that it was ok to still love her dad if she felt she did,
but <u>hate what he had done.</u>
I was going to see her father in prison. Would she like
me to say something to him or would she like to write
something to him which I could give him?
Felicity opted to write but asked me to help her.
She thought about it very carefully and together we wrote: -

"Dear Dad – Mrs. Smith is helping me write this letter because
I don't really know what to say to you. I loved you very much
and trusted you to take good care of me but you didn't.
I told you I didn't really like what you were doing, but you said
it was because you loved me and I mustn't make my sister

74

jealous Now we are all sad and might lose our house. I'm a bit sorry that you are in prison but it is all because of the wrong **you** did, not me. It is your fault and I am not to blame."

We read it through together and Felicity seemed to draw herself up taller and said that she wanted him to see it. I promised her that he would and that he might write a reply to her if she would like that. She nodded.

I visited the man in prison.　　　He appeared to be a meek and mild individual and looked apprehensive. I explained that I had been helping his daughter, whom he had abused, come to terms with what had happened and that she wanted me to tell him how she felt. I gave him the letter.

He read it quietly, twice, then crumpled into a weeping heap and began to relate how guilty he felt; would never forgive himself and did not know why or how it had happened.

I suggested that it is Felicity he should be addressing his remorse to and not me and asked him if he would like to reply to her letter. If so, he must accept all responsibility and release Felicity from all her blame and guilt.

It was agreed that he would do this with the help of his Probation Officer. The letter would be vetted by prison security then by me, before it was forwarded on to Felicity, thereby ensuring that there was no further attempt by him to share or apportion blame, or to coerce for forgiveness, which would be entirely the choice of Felicity.

The letter was short but full of remorse; telling his daughter that none of what had happened was her fault. He stated that he was her dad and it should not have happened.......... he did not ask for forgiveness.

Felicity duly received the vetted letter and I was told by her mother that it seemed to be a great comfort and relief to her. She took pride in showing it to her mother and sister, resulting in a heart-warming family group hug.

This result was reached by the simple process of 'direct work' with a child rather than questions and tick-boxes.

Using inanimate objects or family trees can enable a child to express their feelings of their family and their place in it without struggling to find the right words.

9

A frustrating Investigation into institutional sexual abuse.

I was asked to undertake a joint investigation, with a social services' social worker, into allegations of sexual abuse in a local authority boarding school for boys with special needs.

An allegation of historic sexual abuse had been made by an adult man against one of the teachers. Initial investigations by the police had prompted several other adult men to come forward with similar allegations.

We were not needed to question the alleged victims but statements were needed to be obtained from the rest of the staff. The accused had been suspended and was on bail. The headmaster had arranged for us to visit him and the staff at a meeting. We walked into an atmosphere of palpable hostility.

Several murmurs could be heard of needing to get to class rather than 'wasting time on malicious lies made by freaks'

We tried to engage members of staff on an individual basis but they had all closed ranks, continued to be hostile and could, or would not give a specific time to meet with us.

We had permission to talk to some of the more able boys who were certainly more co-operative but would not be deemed as able enough to sign statements. The information we collated was verbatim and probably would not be used in court. However, any information on how this sports teacher was behaving would be useful.

During the next three visits we heard from several different sources of some of the bizarre and inappropriate behaviour of the accused with the boys.

He was the sports teacher, very popular with the boys and ran a 'tuck shop' where they could spend some of their pocket money on sweets and drinks. He sometimes gave them extra, telling them not to tell anyone else.

Some of the boys told us, with a lot of giggling and nudging each other, that their name for this shop was (hands coyly over mouth) "the fuck shop"; but would not give us specific information as to why.

We learned that, although against the rules, the sports teacher often invited boys into his private flat in the school, out of school hours, particularly after football matches. He allowed them to use his shower and often helped them dry themselves. Sometimes he apologised for accidentally touching their private area when the towel had slipped.

He paid for, and took the chosen few to football matches. He bought films for them to watch most categorised as not suitable for under 18 yr. olds.

He gave them alcoholic drinks with crisps etc in his flat, but they must tell no one else.

He gave special treats to a boy for oral sex or masturbation. He only treated 'special boys' in that way He befriended one 'special' boy's mother on visiting day and told her that he was looking after her son so she need not worry.

When we asked members of staff their view of these

stories, their collective response was that the boys were lying and they did not wish to discuss it further.

They viewed the sports-master as being somewhat of a saint. He would volunteer to take on the most difficult boys, the ones the other staff members did not want to deal with and in doing so became their hero

Whilst the staff refused to believe that a colleague had taken advantage of his position of trust, it was clear that the sports master had become very skilled at recognising the most vulnerable boys right from the start of their reception into the care of the boarding school.

The tuck shop was an obvious attraction to children and he became well known to boys and staff as being kind and generous. The grooming began at this point.

All of the boys had special needs. Some had been excluded from main-stream education. Some had extreme behaviour problems while others had extreme learning difficulties. Some had been in trouble with the law. Most came from homes where the parent/s had given up on trying to cope.

The sports-master had recognised the frailty and vulnerability of certain boys and went out of his way to introduce himself right at the beginning.

The boys were made to feel special, probably for the first time in their life. They were treated like grown-ups, allowed to see naughty films, drink cans of lager and smoke funny cigarettes. Some were privileged to stay-over but not to tell anyone.

These stories were relayed with a sense of pride. It was almost like the boys were boasting that they were thought to be very special and important and the other boys were jealous.

It would take them until adulthood to fully realise how they had been cheated of their innocence and had had their trust of a revered teacher broken.

That realisation would be accompanied by great anger and a sense of grief and confusion.

They were children with no power who had been groomed into believing that they were special. They didn't give informed consent to being abused and probably were frightened, but reassured that everything was ok

Anal penetration usually results in involuntary erection and pleasurable ejaculation, leading to the victim being very confused, believing that they must have wanted it to happen.

In years to come the realisation of the extent of their abuse may result in their anger being acted out in anti-social behaviour.

Thankfully, the historic abuse allegations were believed and the 'evidence' we had compiled in our report backed up the stories told by previous victims.

The perpetrator was given a very long prison sentence and barred from working with children for the rest of his life.

It is interesting how an allegation of sexual abuse is almost aways initially denied by those nearest to the abuser. It is the most shocking, disgusting allegation to be made against someone you have loved and lived with for many years. A person you think you know better than anyone.

The staff at that school must have closed eyes and ears to what was happening, although some of the boys were very vocal about the sports teacher's extra-curricular activities.

The staff, like some family members, were in complete denial of the possibility of anything untoward happening and closed ranks in order to protect those near them.

10

What/who is a child sexual-abuser?

Most sex offenders appear to follow a pattern which is known as 'The cycle of offending' and has been witnessed in the behaviour pattern of male and female sex abusers of any age.

There is usually an element present of <u>repressed</u> sexual interest in children which has always been kept hidden and well under control in the past.

Perhaps just a fantasy, never acted out, until a trigger sets off the fuse of the destructive Catherine Wheel-like cycle; eventually spinning out of control, gathering momentum and power as it reaches each stage.

11.

An example of a basic model of a child sexual-abuse cycle of offending

Trigger

There are many different types of child-sexual abusers

Entrenched paedophiles are thought to have a distorted belief system.   They will never agree to having done anything wrong as they believe that it is perfectly 'normal' and logical to have sex with a child

They view children as sexual beings who enjoy being touched in a sexual way, so would see no reason why they should change their view or behaviour

This belief may stem from the fact that they were abused themselves as children.

The seriously entrenched paedophile is very manipulative and expert at ensconcing himself into occupations with easy access to children, particularly those with special needs or vulnerabilities.

This distorted belief system probably dates from their own childhood experiences and, in my opinion, it is extremely difficult to convince such a person that their thinking is wrong.

Some potential paedophiles may have suppressed their sexual feelings toward a child, or children, for years, being fully aware that it is not considered to be 'normal' but wrong and punishable.

Then they experience trauma or profound stress in their life which acts as the trigger, breaking down their resistance and resolve, enabling them to convince themselves that it is ok to seek 'solace' with a child who may be offering innocent comfort.

Such perpetrators sometimes deliberately target vulnerable single mothers whom they groom with kindness and unused-to flattery. Trust is gained with unrestricted access to children.

Unfortunately, technology i.e., the abuse of the internet, has now become a vehicle for child exploitation.

Paedophiles' beliefs are re-enforced and encouraged via this media. They can share, with other like-minded individuals, their experiences and photographs/videos of their obscene behaviour with innocent children,

Potential abusers, who have never physically acted out their fantasies of sex with children, may, with the help, encouragement and easy accessibility of the internet, carry out depraved acts behind closed doors and drawn curtains, until this becomes no longer satisfying.

They may then 'progress' to seeking out innocent children via various chat sites where the grooming begins.

'Befriending', posing as young people themselves, gaining trust then coercing them into performing 'mutual' sexual acts.

If the internet becomes boring, the next step is to physically seek out potential victims and the cycle is put into motion once again.

Therefore, any 'treatment' method available in an attempt to <u>prevent</u> child sex-abuse must be worth a try.

12

Treatment of child-sexual abusers

Opinions differ as to the 'treatment' of sex-offenders and it has been expressed by many that they should be locked up and the key thrown away.

However, sex offences rarely carry life sentences and whilst prison may remove abusers from the streets for a while, if they are given no opportunity to reflect and, hopefully, try to change their behaviour, on release from prison they will probably find themselves in the same situation as before.

Another popular solution often put forward is that of castration.

Sex-abuse formulates in the head, not the penis. If that biological organ cannot function, some sex-offenders use other things e.g. bottles, metal instruments etc

Violence using a sexual organ is not really about the desire or need for sex, (*If you hit someone over the head with a rolling-pin, do you call it cookery?*), but is to gain control and dominance and, sometimes, unconscious revenge for disturbing events which happened in the perpetrator's past.

Most child abusers are sentenced to long terms of imprisonment, usually isolated from other prisoners to prevent them being targeted with violence, and spend their days doing very little at great expense to the tax payer.

There had been some movement to offer work with child sex-abuse offenders in prisons by the Probation Department and psychologists but there were long waiting lists so it was going to take a very long time and keeping someone in prison is very costly.

One alternative put forward was that perpetrators be offered the chance to avoid prison by agreeing to being placed on probation and attending a sex-offenders' group. The aim of which was that the perpetrator would be given the opportunity to examine and, hopefully, change their addictive behaviour, while at the same time be made aware of, and fully understand the trauma they had caused to a child and their family.

On a personal level I think the word "treatment" for sex-abusers implies some "cure". I prefer that an abuser is offered challenging 'work' of facing up to the devasting effects of their offending behaviour and the impact on the victim/s.

The Probation Service joined with the NSPCC to tackle work with perpetrators and my team was asked to take part.

We had the experience of working with children who had been the victims of sexual abuse and were able to give them a voice, which perpetrators may not wish to hear.

However, the Probation Service needed a streaming system to weed out those not suitable for group work for various reasons, and also to separate the genuine from the opportunist.

Nevertheless, I personally found it difficult to think of sitting in a room with a group of sex-offenders when I may have recently been involved in an investigation of a child victim or undertaken therapeutic work with that child.

Therefore, I requested to be left out of the group work but agreed to undertake face-to-face work with individuals who had been assessed as unsuitable for group work and this was agreed.

A Probation team had assessed Mr. W'. as being unsuitable for group work due to his mild, introverted demeanour but he still needed to face the enormity of his offending. I agreed to take him on to give him the chance to confront his offence.

Session 1.

Mr. W arrived looking very anxious. He appeared to be a very withdrawn, rather shy, character.

I made us both a cup of coffee, to break the ice and. explained that I was going to take him through his cycle of offending, with his input., in order for him to see the stages he had progressed through

Mr. W expressed feeling nervous but wiling to begin to tell the story leading up to the abuse, starting with his relationship with the child's mother.

He had been in a relationship with the single parent mother, who had two children, for a couple of years. Mr. W felt that he had a good relationship with the girls and their mother.   They appeared to have a good arrangement whereby
he worked during the day and his partner did a night shift, leaving Mr. W to look after the children. This seemed to work well until he lost his job** and became very depressed.

The situation eventually became fraught and strained within the family due mainly to the lack of his income which led to Mr. W and his partner having a dispute over money. She left for work one evening, very angry and without saying goodbye. Mr. W was very low and ended up quietly weeping.

Eight-year-old Lucy noticed and asked him why he was crying and gave him a hug. Mr. W welcomed the comfort and this was the beginning of a nightly ritual whereby Lucy paid him a great deal of attention, eventually sitting on his lap with an arm around his neck.

Mr. W. told of beginning to drink a great deal of alcohol which would fuel his self-pity and depression and, at the same time, would have a disinhibitory affect.

He welcomed the attention of Lucy and on one occasion when she cuddled him, he felt sexually aroused by her closeness and appropriately gently moved her off his lap. At this point Mr. W became very upset and I stopped the work to get him a glass of water.

Once Mr. W had composed himself, I challenged him with the fact that because he had moved Lucy from his lap it was clear that he was fully aware that what was happening was very wrong and should have been a warning to him that he was putting Lucy in a position of potential danger.

Mr. W admitted that at the time he was only worried that she might tell her mother.

He then told of fantasising about Lucy whilst masturbating. He knew it was unhealthy but said he couldn't seem to stop himself. Again, he became upset and as the hour was almost spent, I closed the session

Whilst remaining as professional as possible with Mr. W and offering him some water and verbal empathy at his distress, when driving home that evening after the session, I gave in to the inner rage I had been feeling throughout the session.

I had previously read the file so was already aware of the extent of the abuse. I wound down my window and summing up as much energy as I could and in the foulest language I could muster from my vocabulary, I screamed loudly into the darkness of the night, calling Mr. W names equally as foul.

I felt some relief and release from the anger.

Session 2

Mr. W arrived on time; we had coffee and recapped on the last session. He owned that going through what had happened, even though we had only touched on the very beginning, had upset and depressed him.

Nevertheless, he was keen to continue with his cycle of offending

The situation between Mr. W and his partner had not improved and now he was looking forward to her going to work and spending a lot of time with Lucy, primarily watching TV.   He no longer pushed her from his lap and also encouraged her to kiss him. The inevitable arousal was now being dealt with later by Mr. W masturbating whilst fantasising about Lucy.

Me. Do you have any idea of what Lucy may have been thinking or feeling when being cuddled on your lap?

Mr. W. Not really

Me. I think she would probably not have been particularly worried; it was nice cuddling and getting this attention from dad and such a very young child would not be aware of your arousal. Lucy trusted you, why should she worry?

Mr. W became very fidgety, looked uncomfortable, then tears.

Ten-minute tea break to allow things to sink in and for composure.

It was very evident that as we continued with the cycle, Mr. W was finding it increasingly uncomfortable to relay the events.

The next time he was on his own with Lucy, whilst drinking cans of lager he again encouraged cuddles and kisses. On becoming aroused this time Mr, W placed Lucy's hand on his erection and laughingly said "Look at what you have done Lucy". Lucy said she was sorry; and was told by Mr. W not to worry.

Me: Why do you think Lucy apologised? Mr. W I suppose she thought she had done something wrong.

Me: Did she do something wrong? If not, who did? Mr. W Well I guess she thought she did something naughty

Me: Did she do something naughty?

No Answer

Me: What do you think Lucy felt or thought on touching your erection? A big silent pause then:

I don't really know

Me: I think Lucy apologised because she was confused. You made her think she had done something wrong when you said "Look at what you have done". She wouldn't know what it was she touched.
Lucy had done nothing wrong or naughty. **You had.**

When you, without her consent, put her hand on your erection she must have felt even more confused. In her innocence she didn't know what it was she was touching and puzzled at what she may have done wrong to you to cause the lump

. She was only eight years old and probably had no idea what a penis was and certainly not an erect penis.

How do you feel, hearing that? You were her stepfather, in a position of trust which you abused.
Mr. W sat with his head in his hands, sobbing whilst spluttering I know, I know'.

I was struggling to contain my anger and composure so ended the session.

I relieved my anger on the way home in the same manner as before.

** The trigger

Session 3

The cycle continued to take the expected route.

After the incident of Lucy being coerced into touching Mr. W intimately, he moved onto the secrecy and anxiety stage of the cycle, becoming fearful that Lucy might tell her mother or someone else. He apologised profusely to Lucy, buying her chocolate and little gifts saying it was all a misunderstanding; She mustn't tell anyone because she might be taken into care and he might go to prison.

Lucy, very scared, promised him she would tell no one and, pressurised, not even her mother.   Mr. W described the next few days as him feeling sick with anxiety, really worried that Lucy would tell someone when she was at school and every time the doorbell rang, he froze with fear.

However, Lucy told no-one, so the crisis was over for him. His distorted reasoning reassured him that, if she had told no-one, that meant that she really liked what had happened.   (Here the well documented distorted thinking/rationale of the child sex-abuser)

Having convinced himself that all was well and that Lucy liked what he did, he looked forward to their next time together.

Still using alcohol as a dis-inhibitor, this time he told of 'touching' Lucy. When pushed to explain what this meant, he squirmed in his seat for a while then quietly said 'her privates'.

What happened then?

She cried and said I had hurt her so I stopped.

Pushing him to face, acknowledge and verbally admit what he had done.

Why was she hurting if you only just touched her?

He got up from his seat, clenching his hands and hyper-ventilating until I told him <u>firmly</u> to sit down.

Thankfully he did so and I asked him once more what had he done to hurt her.

Again, a long delay whilst wringing his hands and more shuffling in his seat he quietly admitted to finger-penetrating Lucy's vagina.

At last, he verbalised what he had done.

He admitted feeling really scared, immediately apologised and pleaded with her to keep 'our little secret' otherwise Lucy would be taken away from her mother. He promised her it would not happen again.

When Lucy's mother came home from work, she went into Lucy's bedroom to kiss her goodnight and found her realised quietly crying.

Concerned, her mother cuddled her and asked why she was crying. There was some hesitation then Lucy said she couldn't tell her because "I might get taken away."

Immediately alarmed, Lucy's mother reassured her that she would never let anyone take her away and Lucy, tearfully, told her that her bottom was hurting

On examining her daughter, she was shocked at what she saw and realised that Lucy had been assaulted. Lucy reluctantly told her *'It was Dad'* adding, *'but I hurt him too and made him have a big lump'*

When challenged by Lucy's mother, Mr. W initially denied causing the injury blaming Lucy for inflicting the injury herself, However Lucy was encouraged by her mother to reveal the whole story and Mr. W finally admitted the offences and eventually expressed remorse.

The police were called and Mr. W was arrested.

The last period of our session was a difficult one for me and sometimes a little scary

It was necessary to make Mr. W face, head-on, the enormity of his offence and to re-enforce the physical and emotional damage he had caused to Lucy and her family.

He needed to accept full responsibility for his actions.

Whilst appearing to be compliant, Mr. C was understandably reluctant to verbally acknowledge the seriousness of his offence and at one point when pressed to speak the words out loud, I was concerned that he might become obnoxious or aggressive.

However, we finished on a positive note with me explaining that if he was determined to never abuse another child, he must closely examine the stages on his cycle of abuse and to identify where, in that cycle, he might be able to stop going on to the next stage.

He had already identified one area when his instincts had told him that what he was doing was wrong. He now needed to work on the other stages.

We touched on some possible strategies he could use to break the cycle and/or to ensure he didn't start another one.

These would be re-enforced in on-going work with his probation officer.

This was the second child-sexual-abuser I came across as a quiet, reserved, rather inadequate person with very low self-esteem, whose childhood experiences probably held the key. These would probably be explored by his probation officer in order to help him understand the reasons for his behaviour. He certainly did not present as a predator but an opportunist.

I have to admit that I found it extremely difficult to remain open-minded and non-judgemental in this type of work and, in order to ensure that my professionalism did not become compromised, I requested that, in future, my skills and energy should be focussed firmly on therapeutic work with child victims of abuse, not perpetrators.

My request was upheld

Before I move on to the next phase of my work, I think it is important for me to state that not all child-sex abusers use violence, although any abuse of a child is a violation in itself.

It is also equally important to dispel an unpleasant and destructive myth that all sex offences against male children are perpetrated by homosexual males.

Paedophile doesn't mean homosexual or vice-versa

13

Now for something completely different.

After my retirement from NSPCC and, two years later, my return from Russia, I became a self-employed independent assessor for Family Courts.

A Judge may sometimes request an independent risk assessment when a child is placed in the care of a Local Authority, against the wishes of parents.

14

Assessments 1-2

Case 1

A young woman habitual drug user had given birth to a baby boy who was immediately removed from her and received into local authority care pending adoption.

The child's father, who did not live with the mother, had applied to adopt his son but the local authority social services department had objected.

The Family court Judge requested an independent assessment which I agreed to undertake.

The objections raised by the Local Authority in a written report by a senior social worker were:

1   He had no prior experience of caring for a child.
2   He had come from a family with multiple issues well-known to Social Services
3   His extended family i.e., sisters and their children were also monitored by a social worker.
4   He presented with some learning difficulties.
5   When observed at the local family centre with his baby son where he was practising bathing, he often let the baby slip out of his hands.

6   When talking to the baby he used the same words over and over.

7   There was no-one to look after the child when he was at work.

8   He could not ensure that the mother would not return for the baby

The conclusion of their assessment was that the child would be at risk if Mr. B was allowed to adopt him.   My initial thoughts when reading this report were that none of the issues raised seemed to be life-threatening or even great risk factors. Also, where was the evidence' to support these allegations/concerns?

I spent many hours with Mr. B but can only just touch on some of the work we did together

Having read the copious reports already submitted, I visited Mr. B in his well-cared for flat in a multi-story block. He proudly showed me around all of the clean, tidy and furnished rooms.

He presented as a quietly spoken person, understandingly nervous about what was going to happen. I explained that I was hoping that he would help me get to know a little of his background, his present life and interests and why he wanted to adopt his son.

It was agreed that I would visit him for up to six weekly sessions of an hour or so if he were willing to undertake some in-depth work with me, on the understanding that my assessment might not necessarily be in his favour.

Our first session entailed drawing up a family tree on flip-chart paper spread out on the ground, a well-used method to engage someone in actively taking part in exploring their family background, their perceived place in it and some feelings about that.

This is a much better process than firing questions at someone then writing down answers on a note pad which can only be seen by the writer.

In my experience most participants really enjoyed the experience of the 'open book' and expressed surprise at the memories it could evoke.

Mr. B relayed a story of marital violence in his home due to excessive drinking by his father who never worked. He is the youngest of three children, having two older sisters whom he described as always looking after him and protecting him from their father. His two sisters were often in trouble in school and the family was visited by a social worker.

Mr. B expressed feeling very angry towards his father but was too young and didn't know what to do to help his mother. Both parents have since died.
His sisters have children who are also monitored by a social worker, not because of abuse but what was assessed as poor parenting/inadequate parenting.

Mr. B didn't like school, was bullied and left with no qualifications but found a job as a groundsman which he enjoyed.

His father's severe drinking resulted in Mr. B being determined not to follow in his footsteps and although he may occasionally visit the local pub, he only drinks a half a lager. He enjoys the company he finds there.

This is where he first met Brenda. He was flattered when such a pretty woman paid him attention. Knowing very little about her, they eventually set up home together but the relationship was short-lived as she became bored with her life and with him.

Mr. B described coming home from work many times to find his flat full of strangers who Brenda introduced as her friends. He thought they had all been drinking and because of his experience of his father, he told Brenda that he wanted it to stop.

However, the episodes became increasingly regular and eventually he was told by a neighbour that they were drug parties.

Mr. B naively expressed disbelief at first because he was totally unaware of Brenda's past history of drug taking, but it was confirmed by another neighbour and, when confronted, Brenda packed up all her belongings and left.

He was unaware that she was pregnant and only heard through the grapevine that the baby was up for adoption. Tests have revealed that he is the father. He had mixed feelings but was thrilled to be a father and wants the chance to bring up his son.

After this session, I left Mr. B some questionnaires, having checked that he was literate in view of the comment made in the report of him having learning difficulties. He was literate and numerate.

The questionnaires gave him time and space to think about his answers, rather than being put under the pressure of on-the-spot scrutiny of questions and tick boxes.

The questions were down-to-earth common sense about dangers in the home, cooking food and "what would you do if ……?" Another question was how would he care for the child and hold down his job

The questionnaires were completed and ready for me to check out the next time I arrived. He was aware that all the low electric points would need stoppers and the glass-topped coffee table would have to go. He would need to get child gates and a fire-guard.

He had decided that if he could adopt his son, he would give up his job to become a full-time carer until the boy was old enough to start school and, in the meantime, he had visited the local citizens advice bureau and had returned with information on carers allowance, child benefit and grants for a cot, pushchair etc.

He demonstrated that he had given the questions great in-depth thought and had shown great initiative. This man did not smoke or drink excessively and had never been in trouble by breaking the laws. He sometimes went to the local church hall events and I was able to talk to the local priest who gave him a glowing character reference and offered as much support as was needed.

When permission was granted for his son to spend a day with him, he was able to demonstrate to me how he had prepared, cooked and sieved vegetables for the baby's lunch with a yoghurt for dessert. He also showed competence in changing the child's nappy and clothes. The baby did not once display any anxiety or signs of not being comfortable with his father.

Mr. B was adamant that the child's mother would not be allowed to take their son from his home, although he would consider the possibility of her visiting them but only if the authorities agreed.

Mr. B was also keen to accept the offer of attending a local fathers' group in a Barnardo's family centre in order to share experiences and support.

In response to the concerns raised by the senior social worker, my conclusions were that, whilst he had had no previous child-care experience, Mr. B had demonstrated knowledge and common-sense and willingness to accept advice and support.

Parenting is an unknown skill to most first-time parents. There is no test set or exam to pass. It is usually a case of trial and error and hoping you won't make too many mistakes.

The fact that his extended family was known to Social Services should have no bearing on his ability to care for his son and using that as a reason could be interpreted as prejudice.

The slipping baby episode was easily explained. The child had severe eczema and needed to be covered in an aqueous solution making the job of holding him very difficult.

Using the same words over and over again when interacting with a baby is common practice and not an indication of incompetence.

All of the issues raised by the local authority had no solid evidence to back up any 'risk' concerns and seemed to me to be based on prejudice and misjudgement of character. The court was able to see from the questionnaires completed by Mr. B. that, although he was not highly educated, he was literate, showed good common sense and was dedicated to the task of looking after his small son.

It has aways been considered that a child is best living with a family member, if possible, rather than a stranger.

The conclusion of my report was that Mr. B had co-operated fully with everything asked of him to my satisfaction and had not presented any underlying risk factors.

I believed he would make a competent and caring parent and with all the support offered and accepted by him, I could find no reason for him not to be considered suitable for the adoption of his son.

After all parties concerned had received a copy of my report, the Local Authority withdrew its opposition to Mr B adopting his son.

A year later I was told that Mr. B had diligently attended the fathers' group where he was the oldest dad

He made useful contributions to whatever was happening and the younger fathers looked to him for advice and guidance.

He was doing really well in the role of father.

Encouraging good news for me and, again, lessons to be learnt in not judging a book by its covers but to allow and encourage a person to become engaged in the process of evaluating their skills, thoughts and consequent actions. (Cognitive Behaviour Therapy- CBT) *

However, I acknowledge that unfortunately not many local authority social workers would have had as much time to spend, as I did, on one person.

104

*Cognitive therapy: One type of therapeutic approach developed by American psychiatrist Aaron T. Beck. First expounded by him in the ninety-sixties.

Case 2

This was another case of a baby being removed from its drug addicted mother, Ms S, at birth and being received into local authority care, pending adoption.

The mother was, and had been a drug addict for many years. Eight years previously she had had a baby daughter, Penny, removed from birth who was adopted by her maternal grandparents, the parents of Ms. S.

Her sister who was married with a working husband and three children aged two, five and eight years, had applied to adopt her baby niece and their solicitor contacted me to ask if I could undertake the independent risk assessment requested by the Judge.

This assessment involved many interviews including visiting the maternal grand-parents, their eight-year-old adopted granddaughter, local school, health visitor and social services department, Mr & Mrs Z (potential adoptive parents) along with their three children. There were also discussions with the drug support team and with the baby's mother Ms. S. The background history was that after her first baby was removed and adopted by the maternal grandparents, Ms. S began a campaign of terror against them which had been remorseless over the past eight years. Periodical Incidences relayed to me of bricks being thrown through her parents' window, mud against their front door, screaming and shouting outside their house. The police had been called on many occasions to remove Ms. S. She had been fined and imprisoned but was not deterred.

Ms. S twice tried to run over her mother with a car and had accosted her daughter many times when she had been going to or from school. Penny told me that she was very frightened by these incidences and was always nervously looking around to see if her mother was near, she did not want to have visits to or from her mother.

Mr. & Mrs. Z welcomed my intervention and were very eager to get on with the adoption process. They did not consider that taking on another baby, when they already had three children and the youngest really still a baby, was going to throw up any serious problems. They had already involved their children in discussions as to where the baby would sleep etc and relayed an air of expected excitement.

What would they do if the mother came to their door demanding to see her child? What if she was abusive and upset the children? What if she threw bricks at their window and doors as she had done in the past?

They seemed surprised at these questions but I reminded them of how Ms. S had hounded her own mother, because she had adopted Penny, to the point of deliberately driving into her as well as throwing things at the house, even when her daughter Penny was there, putting her at risk. There was no reason to expect any different reaction from her to her latest loss.

I left them to think about these things and we would discuss them at my next visit. Also, with their permission, I would like to talk to the children on their own at another time. In the meantime, the school had advised that the

Z children were doing well and presenting no problems. They were aware of the issues of Penny's mother and kept a watchful eye on events.

Social Services had no issues with the Z family, neither had the health visitor with the youngest.

The drug support centre had agreed to ask Ms. S to see me and whilst she agreed, she missed our first appointment.

When we eventually met. Ms. S was very hostile, challenging, loud and very angry and clearly very much under the influence of drugs

She was adamant that her sister would never have her daughter and challenged why she should. *"She's already got three why does she want mine?"*

She believed that her family had always been against her. She had lost one child to them and was not going to allow them to have another.

She accepted that her sister and brother-in-law were good and able parents to their own children, but she would make sure that she would never let her have this new baby. How did she think she would be able to prevent this happening?

"I'll get clean.
I'll think of something, don't you worry, and you'd better not say they can have my baby"

I <u>was</u> worried – She had issued a threat; she was like an angry lioness looking for her lost cub, determined to find it, whatever the consequences.

On my next visit to the Z family the parents were eager to tell me that they had found a solution to the issues I had raised. They had decided to install a CCTV system around the house so that they would see Ms. S coming.

I was astounded at their unrealistic, almost naïve, response to a potentially dangerous situation not just for them but for their children.

So, you see her coming, then what?

Some hesitation. They had not thought it through.

We'll Call the police

But the police won't be able to stop her from walking up to the house if she is not breaking the law

Again; hesitation.

"We will tell her to go away and if she doesn't, we will call the police"

With a feeling of despair, I asked them to think of any practical problems they may face with the addition of a very young baby to an already rather full house. Their response was that whatever happened they would cope.

.   How did they think it might affect the other children?

They said the children would be fine and were looking forward to having a new baby in the family.

Feeling increasingly pessimistic at their apparent inability to foresee, and have a plan to deal with, any potential danger, I moved on and asked to see the two eldest children. Two-year old Hannah would not fully understand, so she stayed with her mum in another room.

Peter and Jayne sat down, a little apprehensive. I asked them what they thought about a very little baby coming to live with them in their house as part of their family. Peter thought it would be good and Jayne agreed, adding that she would help mum look after her.

I had brought with me my old tin of buttons which I had used on many occasions to help children explain their family and maybe their feelings.

Peter and Jayne looked curiously at the buttons. I tipped a pile out onto the table and asked Peter to pick out a button for everyone in their house whilst Jayne watched and could agree or disagree.

There was great interest. Peter picked a square leather button for dad, a small shiny one with a shank on the back which allowed it to wobble for mum, then three for him, Jayne and Hannah

Jayne changed the 'Jayne' button for a bright red one. I then asked Peter to place his family where he thought they should be.

Dad was placed first, mum by his side, Hannah was placed on top of Mum;(Peter explained that she was sitting on Mum's lap). Peter stood next to Dad and Jayne next to Mum.

Well, that is a very interesting story you have told Peter. Do you feel comfortable with that picture? How about you Jayne.?

 Peter looked very pleased and said he liked being next to Dad.

 Jayne moved her button to be a little closer to Mum and Hannah

Ok, well done. Now can you pick a button for the new baby and show me where she will be if she comes to live with you?

Jayne dived into the button box excitedly before Peter could and pulled out a little round pearl which she held up to show Peter, who nodded. Jayne removed the Hannah button from their mother's lap, placed it on the table a little away from the others and replaced it with the little pearl

The buttons sculpt spoke volumes.

Oh dear – where is Hannah?

Silence: Peter picked up Hannah and, moving Jayne a little aside, put Hannah in between their mother and Jayne. *Well, that's a very interesting but different picture now. How do you think Hannah will feel if the baby takes her place on Mum's lap and, Jayne, how do you feel about making space for Hannah between you and Mum?*

The atmosphere changed. Both children looking pensive and slightly anxious.

What do you think Peter?

Well, I Spec Hannah won't like that, she'll probably cry and scream

Jayne? What about you? She shrugged

'she's <u>always</u> with Mum'

Well, I'm sure there's plenty of love to around in this house for all of you and the baby might not come here to live, so no more worries. Thank you for your lovely button picture – you both did really well, did you enjoy doing it.

A spontaneous *YES*

Having collected as much information as was available, I now had the task of sifting, collating and evaluating the result.

If adoption is considered to be in a child's best interest, the first option has always been to try to place the child with a family member if at all possible.

The atmosphere in the Z family was one of warmth and relaxed close-knit happiness. The three children were vert chatty and friendly with no obvious inhibitions. They were well dressed and well nourished

The family was unknown to Social Services and no concerns had been expressed by their school or heath visitor. The Z family seemed to be the obvious ideal placement solution for their baby niece.

However, Mr. and Mrs. Z's enthusiasm to adopt the baby seemed to have blinded them to the changes that were bound to affect them and their children. It was clear that they had only discussed the positives, perhaps believing there would be no negatives.

They certainly did not seem to have any idea of the probable emotional impact on their three children, not only from the introduction of another child to share the attention and love of their parents but also, more dangerously, on the possible trauma they could experience from the erratic behaviour of the baby's mother.

Their response to my question as to what they would do should Ms. S come to their house to see her baby, seemed to me to be naïve and totally unrealistic' in not acknowledging the danger that Ms. S could pose.

The children's response to my question of what they thought of a new baby coming to live with them was as I expected. It sounded exciting and their parents' enthusiasm reassured them all would be well.

However, the buttons sculpt gave them the chance to play-act and non-verbally express what a new baby in the family would actually mean, particularly to Hannah and Jayne.

Whilst acknowledging that the introduction of a new baby into any family could cause resentment on behalf of other children, which in time may be resolved, the Z family children's perception needed to be taken seriously into the equation.

Ms. S had waged an eight-year campaign of violent hostility towards her own mother because she had adopted her daughter Penny, even accosting her own child in a crazed, drug-fuelled state, with no concern shown for Penny's emotional well-being. She was determined to remain in her daughter's world regardless of the costs to anyone.

She had lost another child whom she had thought was her chance to be a mother again

Even if she achieved the improbable goal of getting clean, this would take far too long for it to be of benefit to her baby who was reaching the stage where she needed to make firm attachments.

Ms. S's animal instinct was to seek out and reclaim. She had no regard for the law and would probably never give up as long as she knew where the child lived

113

I had no doubt that she would harass the Z family if they adopted her daughter and by doing so there would now be four children placed at risk of emotional and possibly physical abuse.

Reluctantly and sadly, for the first time in my career, I suggested to a Judge that a child should not be placed with relatives living in the same vicinity as their mother, but rather as far away from her as possible.

15

EPILOGUE

A sad ending to my reflections on a very small sample of the work I undertook in twenty years of social work.

My reflections, whilst highlighting some disturbing past attitudes and poor managerial decision-making, also highlighted many positive changes affecting professional practice

The professional training of social workers, probation officers, some prison officers and police, involving the input of psychology, which is taken for granted at the time of writing this book, was a challenging concept to many at my time in the profession

This resulted in raised awareness and understanding of some of the probable reasons for the mal-treatment of children in particular, as well as the underlying causes of other unacceptable, anti-social behaviour.

Empathy was now perceived as valid as well as there being a need for relevant punitive action.

The NSPCC's progressive move to follow the advice of child abuse enquiries to employ qualified social workers was the catalyst for great change for that charity.

No longer a 'male-dominated' workforce. No more uniforms and peak caps. The 'rigid' term 'Inspector' eventually dropped, resulting in a less punitive and more caring image. The controversial, but brave and innovative, move to co-operate with the Probation Service to work with child-sex-offenders provided a means by which the voices of child victims of sexual abuse, telling of the trauma and confusion they experienced, could be heard by, and hopefully impacted upon, their abusers.

Unfortunately, I am no longer shocked when I hear of yet another case of abuse of a child, or of a child's needless death at the hands of their carers, but I am saddened at having to admit to not being shocked.

When I hear the appalling news, I find myself sighing and saying quietly "So! nothing has changed, nothing has been learnt, nothing surprises me anymore". That is shocking! Unfortunately, children will still die at the hands of their carers in spite of the laws already in force to protect them and to prevent abuse

Causes are many. Lack of resources from Government level, not enough qualified social workers, too-big-to-manage caseloads too soon after qualifying. Lack of adequate management support, inadequate training 'in the field' and, **always,** a lack of proper communication between agencies.

All of the above factors were present at my time of social-work and, unfortunately, are still the same today. But whereas poverty, poor housing plus alcohol abuse were the main factors at the root of family break-down, or leading to child abuse and/or neglect, additional factors gradually became added to the toxic mix; that of the misuse of drugs and the internet

Dedicated social workers, in spite of the dangers they may face,will always continue to strive to help those in need; to offer support to those who wish to take the opportunity

116

offered to change their life-style; to engage victims, whether children or adults, in therapeutic work in order to enable them to regain some control of their own lives, .

"The hand that rocks the cradle is the hand that rules the world" ** Is a poem purported to praise motherhood as the prime force for <u>change in the world</u>

As encouraging as all of this sounds, I believe little can be changed as long as we live in a system which accepts such a divide between those who have and those who have not.   I despair at hearing of the vast sums of money being made by someone kicking a ball around; millions being made for investors; so-called celebrities undertaking degrading challenges involving the miss-use of innocent wild creatures, all in the name of television entertainment for the great general public and to gain further celebratory/notoriety/status and money for themselves.

Why, whilst living in one of the richest countries in the world, is there a need for food banks in this twenty first century?   It makes no sense, making me feel impotent and ashamed to be part of that system.

Perhaps the subject for another book, but not one to be written by this author.

**Wm. Ross Wallace: published in 1865 under the heading 'What Rules the World'
16

Acknowledgements:

My thanks to the NSPCC

1. For affording me the chance to study and further my knowledge of child sexual abuse;
2. for being pro-active in promoting discussion on the much-needed reform of the investigation process.
3. for being instrumental in promoting changes recommended in the Discussion paper
4. for being innovative in the controversial move to offer "treatment' to abusers.

My gratitude to my good friends and neighbours, Pam and Mike Collier for finding the time, in their very busy schedule, to painstakingly proof-read and offer guidance as to how to bring my many drafts to completion.

17

CARING ABOUT AND PROTECTING CHILDREN

Jean. B. Smith. 2023

Printed in Great Britain
by Amazon

28683721R00069